Contents

1 All About Devon — 2

2 Exeter and East Devon — 14

3 The Southern Riviera: Torbay to Plymouth — 30

4 Dartmoor and the Heart of Devon — 46

5 The North and Devonian Exmoor — 62

Resources — 78

Index — 79

1 All About Devon
A blessed county

Devon seems to be a blessed county, a stunningly beautiful place with something for just about everyone. From roaring surf rolling up to vast blindingly white sand beaches, to tranquil, hidden river backwaters.

All About Devon

From high wind-blown moorlands to sheltered, lush ancient woodlands; from quaint historic harbours and thatch-roofed villages to some busy modern towns and cities, there is an enormous diversity crammed within Devon's hilly borders, and all of it leaving plenty of room for the individual to breathe.

From the coasts to its moors, Devon is a highly rural place of rolling hills covered with farmland, moors and woods, much of it quite wild and remote, perfect places to escape the crowds, to have an adventure, do some walking or simply to relax and enjoy the space and peace. Its two coasts (something unusual in itself) are quite different from each other, the north coast mostly facing the Atlantic, quite rugged and surf-bound, the south coast looking onto the English Channel much calmer, home to an assortment of towns, resorts and secluded, calm coves and estuaries.

Across it all is a smattering of towns and villages, mostly quite old, traditional and historic, though with some highly modern pockets, mostly in and around the three modest urban areas of Exeter, Plymouth and Torbay, all of which hug the most sheltered parts of the south coast.

Left: The stunning colour of heather in full bloom, on Aylesbeare Common, near Exeter.

Above: A very bucolic scene, sheep grazing in a field on the slopes of the Haldon Hills, above the estuary of the River Teign, near Teignmouth.

Above: A stormy autumn sky is reflected in a pool on marshy moorland on Gidleigh Common, near Chagford, in Dartmoor National Park.

Above: Storm surf crashes against rocks on Burgh Island, off Devon's south coast.

All About Devon

The lie of the land

Think of Devon and you think of hills; lots of big rolling steep-sided hills, interspersed of course with deep, sheltered valleys. This is undoubtedly a rolling landscape, from the agricultural heartlands to the high massif that is Dartmoor, covering much of central Devon. Within this, there is plenty of diversity, ranging from Dartmoor's rugged granite and boggy moorland landscapes, to the rich red soils of much of south Devon. Most of the land is agricultural, but a significant proportion is covered by woodland, ranging from protected areas of ancient oak and beech, to large conifer plantations given over simply to production of timber.

Dartmoor is the biggest landscape feature of inland Devon, a massive outcrop of granite that has created a range of high moorland hills, its south and east sides gouged into deep, wooded valleys by a number of rivers. This is a wild and rugged place, quite at odds with the rather gentle and homely landscapes of much of lowland rural Devon.

The coasts are at least as varied as the inland landscapes. Along much of the south coast cliffs alternate with beaches and a string of river estuaries, most of the latter draining water from the high hills of Dartmoor and Exmoor, especially the Exe, Dart and Teign. A string of smaller estuaries, such as the Avon, Erme and Yealm, cut through the south Devon district of the South Hams, dividing its already hilly outline up with deep river valleys that even to this day make getting around a little awkward.

By contrast, the north coast is rugged and thinly populated. At its eastern end, the high hills of Exmoor spill across the border from Somerset, setting up a stupendous coastline that includes some of Britain's highest cliffs. To the west of here stretch Devon's main surfing beaches, the magnificent Woolacombe, Croyde Bay and Saunton Sands, all three spectacularly vast stretches of golden sand. In the west, towards the Cornish border, lies Devon's wildest coastline, the rugged rocky cliffs of the Hartland area, facing directly out to the Atlantic Ocean. Offshore lies the wild island of Lundy, ringed by high cliffs, battered by the Atlantic and Devon's only home to puffins.

In the centre of north Devon's coast is the area's one big river estuary, the combined mouth of the Taw and Torridge Rivers, a wide but very shallow expanse of water, bordered along much of its shoreline by vast sand dunes, a place of great natural beauty.

Right: Towering sand dunes give way to a vast expanse of sandy beach at Woolacombe, on Devon's north coast.

Beautiful Devon: A Portrait of a County

Conservation and Devon's wildlife

With such hugely varied rural and coastal landscapes and relatively low population and industrial pressures, it is not surprising that Devon is rich in both protected environments and wildlife. With two national parks, a natural environment UNESCO World Heritage Site, several marine conservation zones and hundreds of nature reserves, there are plenty of natural habitats in which wildlife is able to thrive.

Largest among Devon's protected areas is Dartmoor National Park, covering almost 1000 square kilometres (368 square miles). The park's most important areas for biodiversity are the sheltered valleys, such as those gouged out by the Rivers Teign and Dart, sites of ancient oak woodlands along the river banks, harbouring quite a diversity of species from deer, badgers, dippers and otters through to wood anemones, primroses and the truly wild daffodil, to name just a few.

Above: Red foxes are a very common resident of the Devon countryside, though not that easy to spot.

Above: Otters are found in every one of Devon's river systems, though as with foxes, are very difficult to see.

Above: Dippers are iconic of Devon's clean and fast-flowing moorland rivers, and are frequently seen dashing up- or downriver, or skipping from rock to rock as they hunt for food.

To the north, Exmoor National Park lies mostly in Somerset, but about a third sits within north Devon. Its high hills, deep valleys, dense woodlands and rugged coastline offer quite a patchwork of wildlife habitats. One of the loveliest is the dense valley woodland that lines the East Lyn River at Watersmeet. This is a great place to watch and get close to the normally rather shy dipper, a lovely bird of fast-moving rivers. Exmoor is also renowned for its red deer, and although most of these are found in moorland areas within Somerset, in Devon they can also be seen on the moors to the south of Watersmeet.

On lower ground a number of marshes and rough grasslands (in Devon known as culm) have been protected for their rare species of butterfly, such as the marsh fritillary, and unusual flowers, including bog bean and bog asphodel.

Down on the coasts, some of the estuaries have international protection due to their importance to

Above: Fallow Deer, though an introduced species, have been an integral part of Devon's countryside for a long time, and are often the most easily seen of the county's three deer species.

Top left: The Bog Asphodel is a stunningly lovely flower that blooms across Devon's bogs and marshes during June and July.

Top right: The Cirl Bunting is so rare in the UK that it survives in this country only in a few pockets of south Devon.

Above left: Cormorants are very common marine birds frequently seen along Devon's coasts, typically diving below the water to chase fish before returning to the surface.

Above right: Grey Herons are another very common water bird, both of freshwater and the salty estuaries, regularly seen hunting fish by wading into the shallows.

over-wintering migratory wetland birds. These include almost the whole of the Exe estuary and parts of the Tamar estuary, both places providing winter homes to tens of thousands of wading birds that come here to feed on the mudflats. Birds typically found here include avocets, godwits, curlews, herons, egrets and a host of duck and goose species.

The Jurassic Coast World Heritage Site stretches mainly along the Dorset coast, but its westen section covers Devon's southeast corner, extending from Exmouth to Lyme Regis. Although protected mainly for geological reasons, some parts are important for plant and animal wildlife, sites within Devon including the Axe and Otter river estuaries and the stunning coastal woodlands of the Axmouth-Lyme Regis Undercliff.

Along much of the coastline, quite apart from the usual gulls, such birds as cormorants, oystercatchers and turnstones are common, along with regular sightings of grey seals, the occasional school of dolphins and even basking sharks. Several stretches of coastline have recently been protected as marine

Above: A flock of Dunlin descends onto sandflats in the Exe estuary in search of food. During the winter months, the Exe estuary becomes home to tens of thousands of migratory birds, rightly earning the estuary multiple layers of both national and international conservation protection status.

conservation zones, principally the entire shoreline around Lundy, much of the Hartland coast, and parts of Torbay and Plymouth Sound, all protected for their valuable reefs, homes to an abundance of fish and shellfish.

Beautiful Devon: A Portrait of a County

Town and country

Despite being one of England's largest counties, Devon's population is only about 1.1 million, leaving plenty of space for countryside and open coastline, a large part of the reason for its great beauty. About half the population lives in the three main urban areas, Exeter, Plymouth and Torbay, with the remainder scattered around the countryside and a host of villages and market towns.

All three urban areas nestle on or close to sheltered parts of Devon's south coast, both Plymouth and Exeter long established as important trading centres at the heads of the Tamar/Plym and Exe estuaries respectively. Torbay, on the other hand, is an aggregation of several towns, principally Torquay, Paignton and Brixham, that have grown up along the curving shore of the bay of the same name, following the 19th century inception and growth of tourism. Only Brixham really has any history longer than this, having been an important fishing harbour for several centuries.

Even though it is the county capital, Exeter is the smallest of the three urban areas, though it is currently one of the fastest growing cities in the UK, its increasingly cosmopolitan reputation attracting ever more international high tech companies, particularly since the Meteorological Office relocated to the city in 2003.

Plymouth, on the other hand, bills itself as the Ocean City, playing on its maritime history and its long association with the Royal Navy. To this day, the city hosts one of its main ports.

In north Devon, the main towns are Bideford and Barnstaple, sitting at the heads of the Torridge and Taw estuaries respectively. Nearby, nestling beside the sheltered waters of the main estuary, are the picturesque old fishing villages of Appledore

Above: Plymouth's Sutton Harbour has become one of the city's most popular attractions, both for visitors and locals.

All About Devon

Above: A thatcher hard at work putting a new roof onto a cottage, keeping alive one of Devon's many traditional skills.

and Instow, relatively quiet backwaters compared to the busy tourist attraction of Clovelly further west. Inland, across north and mid-Devon the scattering of mostly small towns such as South Molton, Holsworthy, Okehampton and Tiverton largely service agriculture, the main economic activity in these rural and less touristed areas.

Ironically, despite the fact that many farm workers live a life quite divorced from the world of tourism, it is the farming – and many of the traditional industries that surround it, such as forestry, thatching, hedge-laying and so on – that has the most decisive impact on the Devon landscape, largely creating and maintaining its beauty and making it a place that so many people want to visit.

Similarly, fishermen have created and maintain the attractiveness of the many little harbours that lie along Devon's coasts, today such great visitor attractions, as well as of course supplying much of the seafood for the restaurants. So, it is these two traditional Devon industries that have created much of the Devon that visitors want to see, and which are most visible to visitors.

Above: A fishing boat heads back towards Brixham at the end of a hard day's work.

Above: A street cafe on Exeter's Cathedral Close, with the city's magnificent Cathedral as a backdrop.

Right: One of Dartmouth's most historic landmarks, the Royal Castle Hotel sitting beside the town's inner harbour.

Beautiful Devon: A Portrait of a County

Farming the land

Farming has been at the heart of Devon's economy for centuries. The upper hills of Dartmoor, for example, were settled as long ago as 4000BC, and from at least the Middle Ages onwards it was sheep and their wool that gave wealth to towns like Crediton and Tiverton.

To this day, farming remains critical to Devon, at least in terms of economic output and the amount of the county's land devoted to it. As elsewhere, however, it employs far fewer people than it once did. That said, it remains – directly or indirectly – the lifeblood for a significant proportion of Devon's rural population, particularly among those living in the scattered villages and market towns of mid-Devon.

Above: In a snowbound field near Okehampton, sheep look hopefully towards the photographer for food!

Above: A beautiful oak tree towers over a field of wheat in agricultural countryside near Tiverton.

As any tour of Devon will reveal, its rolling hills are largely a patchwork of relatively small hedge-bound fields alternating with pockets of woodland. The vast hedge-free acres of arable crops that today are such a feature of many other parts of agricultural England, thankfully have had only a relatively small impact on the Devon landscape, the outward appearance, at least, still that of the quintessential bucolic English countryside.

One of the main reasons for the survival in Devon of the traditional farming landscape is because much of the region's agriculture is geared towards animals rather than crops. Most animal husbandry – with the exception of that on the open moors – needs relatively small, well-fenced fields in which to constrain wandering herds and to allow management of grazing.

That is not to say there is no arable farming in Devon; of course there is a considerable amount, but it is on a relatively small scale compared to that in other parts of the UK. Sheep and cattle remain the kings of Devon agriculture, as they have for many centuries. The many summertime agricultural shows that take place across the county are dominated by a surprising diversity of breeds, and the events themselves constitute important cornerstones of the rural communities' economic and social lives.

In recent years many farms have started to diversify into other areas, typically of course into tourism, with campsites and rental cottages, but also into novel products that range from alpacas, to jams and chutneys, to wines. One benefit of global warming is that Devon's climate has become increasingly suited to the cultivation of grapes, allowing for a steadily growing number of vineyards across the county. Though still on a relatively small scale, some vineyards are nevertheless generating a good name for their wines, with one of the most well known being Sharpham Vineyard on the banks of the Dart, and near Totnes.

Fishing the seas

Like farming, fishing is one of Devon's great traditional industries, though today it contributes only a tiny amount to the county's overall economy. While 50 years ago significant fleets of fishing boats would have been found at just about every little harbour along both of Devon's coasts, today most of them have just a handful, if even any at all. Places like Beer, Seaton, Exmouth, Teignmouth and Dartmouth along the south coast, and Ilfracombe, Appledore and Clovelly on the north still each have a few boats that catch mostly crabs and lobsters from networks of baskets (or pots, as they are called) permanently laid out along the seabed, plus some fish from handlines, making mostly just day trips out from their home harbour.

Above: Fishing boats crowd into Brixham's harbour, the busiest in the southwest of England.

Above: Crates of plaice and huss waiting to be off-loaded from a fishing boat, just arrived in Brixham's fishing port.

The larger trawlers, which catch fish with nets, and many of which head out to sea for days at a time, work largely out of just two Devon harbours, Brixham and Plymouth. In addition to the trawlers, some of the boats from these ports catch fish on long multi-hook lines, while dredging of scallops from the sea floor is also common.

Both harbours have wholesale fish markets right alongside the wharves, selling to distributors, stores and restaurants. The general pattern is for the boats to land their catch in the evenings, with the fish sorted during the night, and then auctioned in the market from about 6am onwards.

Despite the general decline in fishing over the past decades, at present both Brixham and Plymouth seem to be doing quite well. Not just the volume of seafood, but also the diversity of species for sale in the market is quite astounding, ranging from the usual mackerel and pollack through large numbers of flatfish such as plaice, brill, turbot, John Dory, and lemon and dover sole, to hake, bass, gurnard, pouting, dogfish, monkfish, ling, conger eels, squid, cuttlefish, skate and mountains of scallops. To someone who loves seafood, it is all quite a mouth-watering sight!

Beautiful Devon: A Portrait of a County

Devon's tourism

Devon is without doubt one of Britain's most popular holiday areas, so not surprisingly tourism is huge in the county. Millions of people flood into Devon every year, at peak holiday times more than doubling the population, drawn by the beautiful countryside and coastal scenery.

Most visitors head for the coast, especially the spectacular surfing beaches of the north coast and the string of relatively small beaches that line Torbay. Other popular beaches include the many lovely white sand coves along the south coast in the South Hams area, especially such places as Blackpool Sands near Dartmouth and (further west) the stunning twin beaches of Bantham and Bigbury, separated from one another by the sandy Avon estuary. The beaches of east Devon are popular too, though most of these are shingle, the exception being the long sandy stretch of Exmouth beach.

Not surprisingly, this is really the place for watersports. That great Exmouth beach is ground zero for Devon's kite-surfing and windsurfing, with quite literally dozens of boards out on a good windy summer's day. Bantham too, is a hugely popular

Above: With its beaches exposed to the Atlantic swell, north Devon is one of Britain's most popular surfing areas, seen here at Croyde Bay.

place, though a little less easy to reach than Exmouth.

On the north coast, the larger waves mean that surfing is king here, with Saunton Sands, Croyde Bay and Woolacombe all popular spots for both beginners and experts alike, with hired boards, wetsuits and tuition all readily available.

When it comes to boating, fishing trips are widely available, as are boat tours between many of the harbours. It is also often possible to hire and self-skipper boats, both with and without sails. When it comes to yachts and dinghy sailing, Torbay, Plymouth, Salcombe and Dartmouth are all major centres.

Some of the most popular towns include those of Torbay, Torquay and Paignton for their beaches and cafes, Brixham for its busy fishing harbour. Dartmouth, Salcombe and Plymouth are popular too for their historic and highly scenic harbours. Towns like Sidmouth, Dawlish and Teignmouth attract people for their traditional seaside ambience, while the inland town of Totnes attracts people for its name as an artistic community.

On the north coast, Ilfracombe also has the traditional seaside ambience, while perhaps the biggest draw of all is the impossibly picturesque

Above: A revolutionary new hydrofoiling windsurfer, lifting completely clear of the water, flies along off Exmouth, today one of the southwest's leading windsurfing and kite-surfing venues.

All About Devon

Above: The picture postcard village of Clovelly, clinging to the steep slopes of the north Devon coast, has been receiving hordes of visitors for a long time, and is still one of the county's big attractions.

Above: An early morning view across the River Dart from Dartmouth towards Kingswear.

Above: A dusk view of one of the many restaurants that line the quayside of Sutton Harbour, in Plymouth.

Above: An accordion player leads a group of morris dancers, at the famous annual Sidmouth Folk Festival.

village of Clovelly, clinging tightly to a precipitous coastal hillside west of Bideford. Its single cobbled street (strictly no vehicles here), drops steeply downhill between rows of lovely cottages to a perfect little fishing harbour, the quintessential *ye olde* fishing village.

In the Devonian part of Exmoor, the main attractions lie along the coast, particularly at Heddon's Mouth and the twin villages of Lynton and Lynmouth, with their lovely wooded Watersmeet and the spectacular Valley of Rocks.

The main inland attraction is undoubtedly Dartmoor, which typically receives thousands of day visitors during the main holiday seasons. Most tend to simply drive around to admire the lovely views and the moor's famous ponies, so while the traffic can be trying, anyone prepared to park up and start walking will quickly leave the crowds behind and end up with the moors virtually to themselves. And there is some truly fabulous hiking to be had on Dartmoor, both out on the open moors and in the valley woodlands.

So, with this introduction to the beauties and attractions of Devon, all that is left to do is get out there and explore...! Enjoy the following photoessays as a guide to this beautiful Devon.

2 Exeter and East Devon

This is the land of Devon's booming cosmopolitan capital, rich red farmland soils and a coastline that forms the western end of the magnificent Jurassic Coast World Heritage Site.

The wide, shallow expanse of the River Exe estuary establishes a natural border to the region, separating east Devon from the south, Torbay and Dartmoor, the estuary's head creating a convenient hub that is today's city of Exeter.

Though an important Roman centre, at that time called Isca, it was following the Norman conquest that its longterm role was sealed with the 12th to 14th century construction of the magnificent cathedral. To this day, the cathedral remains right at the city's heart, both historic and modern. Despite the presence of a cathedral, for much of history Exeter has been rather a quiet backwater, but in recent years its economy has boomed, drawing in businesses and people from around Europe, giving it an increasingly international flavour.

Along the Exe estuary, immediately south of Exeter, sits a place that harks back to a previous international era; the lovely riverside village of Topsham, once a transhipment harbour for goods going to and from the city. To this day, some of its oldest streets are lined with houses built in Dutch architecture, a remnant of the 17th century days when Topsham traded extensively with the Netherlands.

Right at the river's mouth sits the town of Exmouth, once a port but now - thanks to its stunning sandy beach - a major holiday destination. It is also one of the southwest's biggest hotspots for kite-surfing and windsurfing, enthusiasts attracted from far and wide by its good winds and protected waters.

Heading east along the coast from Exmouth, the nearby Orcombe Point marks the start of the Jurassic Coast World Heritage Site, the coastline protected for its international geological importance, and stretching all the way to Studland Bay, just short of Poole Harbour. Here in east Devon, the cliffs are a

Above: Exeter Cathedral is one of Britain's oldest cathedrals, and almost certainly the southwest's most historic building. The centrepiece of its interior is the spectacular nave. Not only does it run the entire length of the Cathedral, but it has the longest uninterrupted medieval vaulted ceiling in the world.

strikingly rich red colour, the Jurassic Coast's oldest rocks, dating from the Triassic Period over 200 million years ago.

Along much of this coast the cliffs are surprisingly high and sheer, but here and there they drop down to sea level to create the occasional cove, such as Branscombe, as well as leaving space for a number of well known resort towns, including Budleigh Salterton, Sidmouth, Beer and Seaton.

The red soils continue inland, with rich hilly farmland that merges into the Blackdown Hills, protected as an Area of Outstanding Natural Beauty. This is one of Devon's most intensively agricultural regions, though of course a number of towns lie scattered across this area including Ottery St Mary, Axminster and Honiton. Today, all three are thriving market towns, and Honiton was once famous for its fine lacemaking.

Left: An atmospheric sunset view across the River Exe at Topsham, a quintessential Devon evening view. Topsham is a very historic village and one-time trading port at the head of the Exe estuary, just south of Exeter.

Beautiful Devon: A Portrait of a County

Above: The magnificent south side of Exeter Cathedral, lit up by a golden winter evening sunlight. Built in the 12th–14th centuries, Exeter's is one of Britain's oldest cathedrals, a grand and beautiful example of (at least partially) Norman architecture.

Above: One of the oldest surviving fragments of historic Exeter, a diminutive wood-framed medieval house and the delightful 15th century St Mary Steps church tower, complete with its 17th century musical clock, that stand alongside Stepcote Hill on the hillside just above the River Exe.

Left: Not surprisingly, the focal point for many of Exeter's historic buildings is around the Cathedral, and in particular along Cathedral Close, the lane that marks the edge of the green on the Cathedral's northern side. Most of the buildings here are several hundred years old, including these Medieval buildings.

Exeter and East Devon

Left: One of Cathedral Close's most historic Medieval buildings is topped by a small observatory, today appropriately the headquarters of the Devon and Exeter Institution.

Above: On Exeter Cathedral's northern side is a statue of Richard Hooker (1554–1600), a leading theologian who was born in Heavitree, today a district of Exeter, and educated at Exeter Grammar School and Corpus Christi College, Oxford.

Above: Swans are a major, and very popular, feature of the River Exe as it flows past the old Exeter Quay, ever eager to get in line for a few free food handouts.

Beautiful Devon: A Portrait of a County

The most striking elements of Exeter's modern architecture are – perhaps not surprisingly - largely commercial, as evidenced by these three photos, where overall shape, line, angle and stark simplicity are the key features, in total contrast to the complex details commonly found in the historic buildings.

Above left: The criss-crossing lines in the glass wall and escalators of the John Lewis department store.

Above right: Sharp angles and a gentle curve in the walls above the Princesshay shopping centre.

Left: The soft, almost seductive curves of the Next store.

Right: Not really on public show, but nevertheless one of Exeter's most architecturally striking modern buildings is the national headquarters of the Meteorological Office. When Britain's weather service moved its head office from Bracknell to Exeter in 2003 it delivered a major economic boost to the city, pointing the way towards the city's growth as an important modern business and technological hub.

Exeter and East Devon

Above: The facades of some of Topsham's most historic buildings, 17th century Dutch-style houses built along the Strand, running close to the shore of the Exe estuary. At the time these houses were built, Topsham was a hugely important port, exporting Devon's wool to the Netherlands, the ships bringing back tiles and bricks simply as ballast in what would otherwise have been empty ships. These materials then went into the building of these houses.

Right: A detail of the gables and facade of one of Topsham's Dutch houses, lit up by evening sunlight.

Left: Although Topsham stopped being an important trading port many years ago, today it still retains a strong maritime atmosphere, the river close by filled with moored yachts, and the shore lined with all kinds of craft, including a number of old boats in the throes of restoration.

21

Beautiful Devon: A Portrait of a County

Exeter and East Devon

Above: The lovely riverside village of Lympstone seen in evening sunlight. An historic old seafaring village lying on the Exe estuary's eastern shore, between Topsham and Exmouth, Lympstone's old houses crowd in very tightly around its tiny harbour. Rather a quiet backwater these days, the name 'Lympstone' is more closely associated with the adjacent Royal Marine Commando training centre than it is with this quaint little village.

Right: The remains of a disintegrating old wooden barge, left in the shoreline mud at Turf Lock, close to the entrance to the Exeter Canal, makes for an eerie outline on a foggy morning. As shipping on the Exe declined in the 20th century, so many old barges like this one were simply abandoned, leaving such wrecks quite commonplace.

Left: One of Topsham's most beautiful and most cared-for Dutch-style houses, a feature of the shoreline Strand, made even lovelier in early summer by its wisteria in full bloom.

Beautiful Devon: A Portrait of a County

Left: Not surprisingly, messing about in boats comes high on the agenda for activities in and around the Exe estuary. Here, a dinghy is caught racing on the estuary's sheltered waters, out from Starcross Yacht Club, one of Britain's oldest yacht clubs but today one of the southwest's most competitive centres for sailing dinghy racing.

Right: Exmouth's beach, just outside the mouth of the River Exe, has become arguably the southwest's leading centre for windsurfing and kite-surfing. A typical weekend in summer will see upwards of 50 boards out sailing on Exmouth's sheltered waters at any one time, quite a colourful and exhilarating sight.

Below: Exmouth's harbour, sitting just inside the mouth of the River Exe, was at one time a busy commercial port. But with shipping declining from about the 1970s onwards, the port eventually fell into disuse. Today, it has a new lease on life, the harbour now a crowded marina, its warehouses replaced by modern and upmarket housing.

Beautiful Devon: A Portrait of a County

Right: The seafront at Sidmouth, a place that has a reputation for being a rather staid type of resort left over from another era, but which in fact has quite an attractive, if quaint town centre, and which attracts tens of thousands of visitors during its annual Folk Festival.

Below right: Early morning sunlight illuminates woodland bluebells, one of Britain's icons of early summer, seen here at Blackbury Camp, the remains of a prehistoric hilltop village, close to today's Beer on Devon's southeast coast.

Above: The beautiful Palm House at Bicton Park Botanical Gardens. Built in the 1820s, it has an iron framework and a staggering 18,000 panes of glass. Completed some 20 years before its larger cousin at Kew Gardens, in London, some believe the Bicton Palm House to have been a deliberate prototype for the Kew structure.

Exeter and East Devon

Below: A morning silhouette of the mighty cliffs that consitute Beer Head, one of highest and most rugged headlands in the western part of the Jurassic Coast World Heritage Site, seen here from the beach at Branscombe..

Above: Silhouettes of fishing boats pulled up onto the beach at Beer. Beer is unusual in that it has a still-active fishing fleet despite having no harbour, the boats having to be hauled up high onto the steep shingle beach every time they come ashore. The boats here catch mainly high value shellfish, from crabs to scallops.

Below: A calm and peaceful dusk view of the estuary of the River Otter, just before it reaches the sea at Budleigh Salterton. As can be seen here, the estuary weaves its way through a coastal marsh before joining the sea. Upstream from here, the River Otter has gained fame as the first reintroduction point for European Beavers back into the wild in England, an experiment that so far seems to be going very well.

Beautiful Devon: A Portrait of a County

Agricultural shows are a very important part of the social calendar for many of Devon's rural communities, and this is nowhere more so than in east Devon. Not only is the Devon County Show held every May just east of Exeter, but later in the summer the Honiton Show focusses quite specifically on east Devon's farming community, highlighting some of the best agriculture the area has to offer.

Left: The Devon County Show in particular shows off not just livestock but also traditional skills, such as in the blacksmiths' horse-shoeing contests.

Above: The more intimate Honiton Show gives everyone a chance to get really close to some of the animals, whether they be small children with sheep, or – **Below** – an owner tending to her young bull.

Exeter and East Devon

Quite apart from the agricultural shows, east Devon has more than its fair share of many other festivals that get wide attention and draw in the crowds. During the summer, the leading event is the Sidmouth Folk Festival, during which not only are fixed venues sites for a host of performances, but the entire seafront becomes one big open-air buskers' heaven, with free performances constantly on show along its length.

Top left: A duo of guitarists entertain more or less just themselves, along with anyone willing to stand and listen.

Above: More demanding of attention is a one-man band, playing to the crowd.

Above left and left: A rather crazier event is the annual Ottery Tar Barrels, held in Ottery St Mary every Guy Fawkes Night. Instead of fireworks, the people of Ottery opt to carry blazing barrels caked with tar through the town's streets, the carriers generally running at full speed through the crowds. It is quite an experience, though not for the faint-hearted!

3 The Southern Riviera
Torbay to Plymouth

Stretching all the way from Dawlish in the east to Plymouth in the west, this southern coastal area is the heart of Devon's tourism, the main magnet for the great majority of visitors to the county, if not the whole of the southwest.

Although the term 'Riviera' applies strictly speaking to just Torbay, the great beauty of this coast makes it quite applicable to virtually the whole area.

It is also the most populous part of Devon, with towns scattered along much of its length. Plymouth is by some margin Devon's largest city, and even Torbay has a larger population than Exeter. Plymouth is largely a working city, one with a long-held naval heritage and to this day one of the UK's main naval bases. Its tourism attractions lie mostly around the historic shoreline at the Hoe, the Barbican and Sutton Harbour, all closely tied to major events in British history.

In stark contrast to urban Plymouth, the South Hams, the area between Plymouth and Brixham, is intensely rural, with just a handful of small towns, principal among which is the historic and artistic centre of Totnes. For the most part, however, the South Hams is a place of small impossibly picturesque villages of thatched cottages, linked by a spider's network of infuriatingly narrow lanes that are the bane of visiting drivers. Getting around this area can take time and patience, but the rewards are a seemingly endless series of beautiful river estuaries and sandy beaches. This is the quintessential Devon coast, much of it protected within both the South Devon Area of Outstanding Natural Beauty and the South Devon Heritage Coast.

To the east of the South Hams, Torbay is largely built up, consisting mostly of the towns of Torquay, Paignton and Brixham, which along with a number of smaller places have merged into what is nearly a single urban area, nestling around the beautiful shores of the sweeping arc of Torbay itself. Along with the resort towns of Dawlish and Teignmouth on Torbay's northern fringes, this is really the hub of south Devon's tourism, attracting many thousands

Left: A dusk view of the harbour and ferris wheel at Torquay, the focus of much of Torbay's tourism, and increasingly one of Devon's iconic views.

Above: Surfers head for the waves at Bantham, on Devon's south coast and in the heart of the South Hams district. Although the north Devon coast gets most of the surfing action, the west-facing, rather exposed coast at and around Bantham frequently sees good surf.

of visitors every year, who come for the area's hotels, beaches and nightlife.

Though parts of this Riviera region are quite urbanised, most of it consists of stunningly beautiful rural and coastal scenes, and it is these - the estuaries, beaches, cliffs, rolling farmland and quaint villages - that are the main attractions for the vast majority of visitors. This is the quintessential Devon.

Beautiful Devon: A Portrait of a County

Above: Lit by golden sunlight on a calm evening, the Torquay shoreline fronted by the classy, glistening boats of the marina, has an almost Mediterranean feel to it, giving credibility to the 'Riviera' tag applied to this part of the south coast. It is a view that has certainly attracted many people to the Torbay region.

Left: While most of the Torbay area has grown up on the tourism industry of the past 150 years, Brixham, sitting at the southern end of the bay, has a history going back many hundreds of years, centred mostly on its role as an important fishing port. To this day, it remains central to the south coast's fishing industry, the southwest's busiest fishing harbour.

The Southern Riviera: Torbay to Plymouth

While much of Brixham harbour is devoted to its modern fishing industry and its yacht marina, there is a segment dedicated to the restoration and sailing of historic old sailing trawlers, such as *Pilgrim* and *Vigilance*, two old sailing work boats that are well known to Torbay's boat-loving community. The masts and rigging of these and other boats lend an historic and traditional seafaring touch to Brixham's busy harbour scene, providing a sense of continuity between the past and present. Photographically, they are wonderful boats to explore, with their criss-crossing lines, big chunky wooden blocks, **(above)**, beautifully curving wooden hulls and sturdy bowsprits **(left)**.

Bottom: Never ones to miss an excuse for some fun, Brixham's fishing crews throw themselves enthusiastically into the annual Brixham Trawler Race, held every June. The trawlers race around a roughly triangular course, the boats divided into several fleets according to size and engine power. It is not clear if anyone cares who wins: it is simply an excuse for a party.

Beautiful Devon: A Portrait of a County

The Southern Riviera: Torbay to Plymouth

Left and above: Paignton is the archetypal British seaside holiday resort, a long seafront backing a nice sandy beach, a pier stretching out to seawards, beckoning as an excuse for a walk, and giving great views back to the beach from its outer end, these days dominated by a small funfair. At dusk, the pier comes into its own, lit up and becoming quite magical.

Below: Rather more sedate is the jetty-cum-boardwalk that encompasses the southern edges of Torquay Marina, enticing visitors to take an evening stroll out over the water to take advantage of its wonderful views across the harbour and along the coast.

Above: Grapes being picked in the autumn at Old Walls Vineyard, in Bishopsteignton, near Teignmouth. Farming may not be easy these days, but one benefit of global warming is the increasing possiblity for farmers to diversify into such luxury products as wine, something that even south Devon just did not have the weather to manage 30 years ago.

Above: A low winter sun silhouettes one of the many groynes that line and stabilise the beach at Dawlish Warren. The Warren is a long sandy spit that cuts across much of the mouth of the River Exe, sheltering the estuary from the open sea. Were it to disappear then the whole of the estuary – and the towns along it – would be seriously exposed. When storms in February 2014 almost breached the Warren this did become a possibility, massively highlighting the importance of Dawlish Warren's sea defences.

Above: A peaceful evening on the estuary of the River Teign, seen from Shaldon, on the southern shore of the estuary. Like the Exe, the mouth of the Teign is protected by a sandy bar, though this one is stablised by having the town of Teignmouth sitting on it!

The Southern Riviera: Torbay to Plymouth

Right: The normally quiet and laidback village of Shaldon, sitting in the mouth of the River Teign, bursts into life every August for its slightly zany annual Water Carnival, a day when its river mouth harbour fills with colourful floats designed to entertain, amuse and often ultimately sink. This particular float, created from several boats tied together, was intended as a homage to the rock band Queen.

Below: The very mouth of the River Teign, seen from the Teignmouth shore, is punctuated by the iconic Ness, a huge sandstone rock and cliff that marks the very end of both the river mouth and the village of Shaldon.

Beautiful Devon: A Portrait of a County

Right: The sands of Bigbury-on-Sea, on the coast of the South Hams, form a vast expanse at low tide, but so shallow is the beach's slope that the tide races in at quite a speed, quickly gobbling up and submerging much of the beach, including the sandbar that stretches across to adjacent Burgh Island.

Below: Historic Bayard's Cove, a small wharf lined with 15th and 16th century buildings, is one of the most historic, and most famous parts of lovely Dartmouth, sitting – not surprisingly – just inside the mouth of the River Dart. Truly the quintessential *'ye olde'* English harbour – except that it is the genuine article - the Cove has been used in many film shoots and television dramas.

The Southern Riviera: Torbay to Plymouth

Above: With its deep water estuary harbour (the water remains deep even at the lowest of low tides), easily protected and guarded through the high cliffs that line the river mouth, Dartmouth has been at the heart of Britain's naval tradition since at least the time of Henry VIII. Dartmouth Naval College, sitting on the hillside above the town and estuary, is where the Royal Navy's officers are trained, a site that has been used for this purpose since 1863.

Left: As with this cottage in the village of Hope, the South Hams district is typified by villages of impossibly quaint, thatch-roofed houses, many of them centuries old. Once upon a time they were the homes of the poorest rural farm labourers. Today, many are among the most comfortable and upmarket of holiday homes, an integral component of Devon's attraction.

Beautiful Devon: A Portrait of a County

Above: The bustling town of Totnes, site of a Norman castle, a section of town wall and the town gate, is both an historic place and one famous for its arts and rather alternative lifestyles, built up around the (now sadly closed) nearby Dartington Art College, something that makes this south Devon town really quite unique.

Above: Bathed in a soft evening sunlight, boats crowd around one of Salcombe harbour's many pontoons.

Below: In the old village of Noss Mayo, sitting on the shores of the River Yealm estuary, cottages crowd in close to the shore. It is something of a heaven for boating enthusiasts, and a place that – rather hidden down narrow country lanes – is off the main tourism beaten path.

The Southern Riviera: Torbay to Plymouth

Above: A dusk view of the lovely village of Salcombe, sitting on the shores of the Kingsbridge Estuary, actually not a river estuary at all but simply a drowned valley. Salcombe and the lovely estuary is one of Devon's most popular visitor attractions, though this particular view, being a little hard to reach, is one that few people get to see.

Right: A sunset view of Start Point and its lighthouse, one of Devon's most prominent and most rugged headlands, pointing eastwards well out into English Channel, and forming the southernmost limit of the huge Lyme Bay, which stretches all the way north to Dorset's Portland Bill.

Beautiful Devon: A Portrait of a County

Above: The Mayflower Steps, next to the Barbican and Sutton Harbour in the historic heart of Plymouth. In 1620, the Pilgrim Fathers left from this spot to sail across the Atlantic and set up the first English colonies in the New World. Their brave journey is still commemorated here today with this plaque and ceremonial gateway.

Right and above right: A visiting square-rigged tall ship sits in Sutton Harbour, site of Plymouth's original harbour, recalling, continuing and emphasising Plymouth's long-held and historic association with the sea and seafaring.

The Southern Riviera: Torbay to Plymouth

Above: The Barbican is Plymouth's most historic district, an area of ancient buildings sitting between the city's original harbour and the nearby hilltop Citadel (still a military base). All the buildings here are old, some – such as this one – dating from the 16th century and the first Elizabethan era.

Below: Much of the Barbican is filled with bars, restaurants and pubs, many recalling the district's tight involvement with the sea, including the pub attached to this sign, the Ship Inn, one the Barbican's oldest inns.

Above: A total contrast to the ancient buildings of the Barbican, the ultra-modern glass walls of the National Marine Aquarium, stand on the opposite side of Sutton Harbour, reached from the Barbican by walking across the lock gates that close off the inner harbour from the tides of the open sea. A Millennium project that opened in 1998, the Aquarium showcases some of the submarine life that can be seen around the southwest's coasts, from sharks to cod and much more besides. It is undoubtedly one of Plymouth's star attractions not only for local school groups but visitors from around the country.

Beautiful Devon: A Portrait of a County

Right: The Royal William Yard was once a major Royal Naval supply centre, which was decommissioned only in the 1990s. Now slowly being transformed into a combined yachting harbour and restaurant/bar district, the Yard is steadily attracting more and more people, and is likely to become another visitor focal point along Plymouth's shoreline.

Below: The magnificent Tinside Lido is a wonderful outdoor swimming pool built along the shore beside Plymouth Hoe. Neglected and looking rather sorry for many years, recent renovation has restored the Lido to its former glory, work that has been amply rewarded by the huge numbers of people that flock to it on a good summer's day.

The Southern Riviera: Torbay to Plymouth

Right: Smeaton's Tower dominates Plymouth Hoe, for many years one of Plymouth's most famous landmarks. No longer a functioning lighthouse, it was the third Eddystone Rock lighthouse, protecting shipping from this dangerous offshore rock for nearly 100 years from the middle of the 18th century. In the latter part of the 19th century a new Eddystone lighthouse was built, and this one – named after its engineer – was moved to Plymouth Hoe in 1882.

Below: Every summer Plymouth hosts the British Fireworks Championships, providing two evenings of spectacular fireworks displays, fired off from the Mountbatten breakwater close to the inner shore of Plymouth Sound – the bay that fronts onto the city – and viewed by huge crowds from nearby Plymouth Hoe. In the view shown here, a nearly full moon can be seen rising above the horizon just as one of the displays reaches its climax.

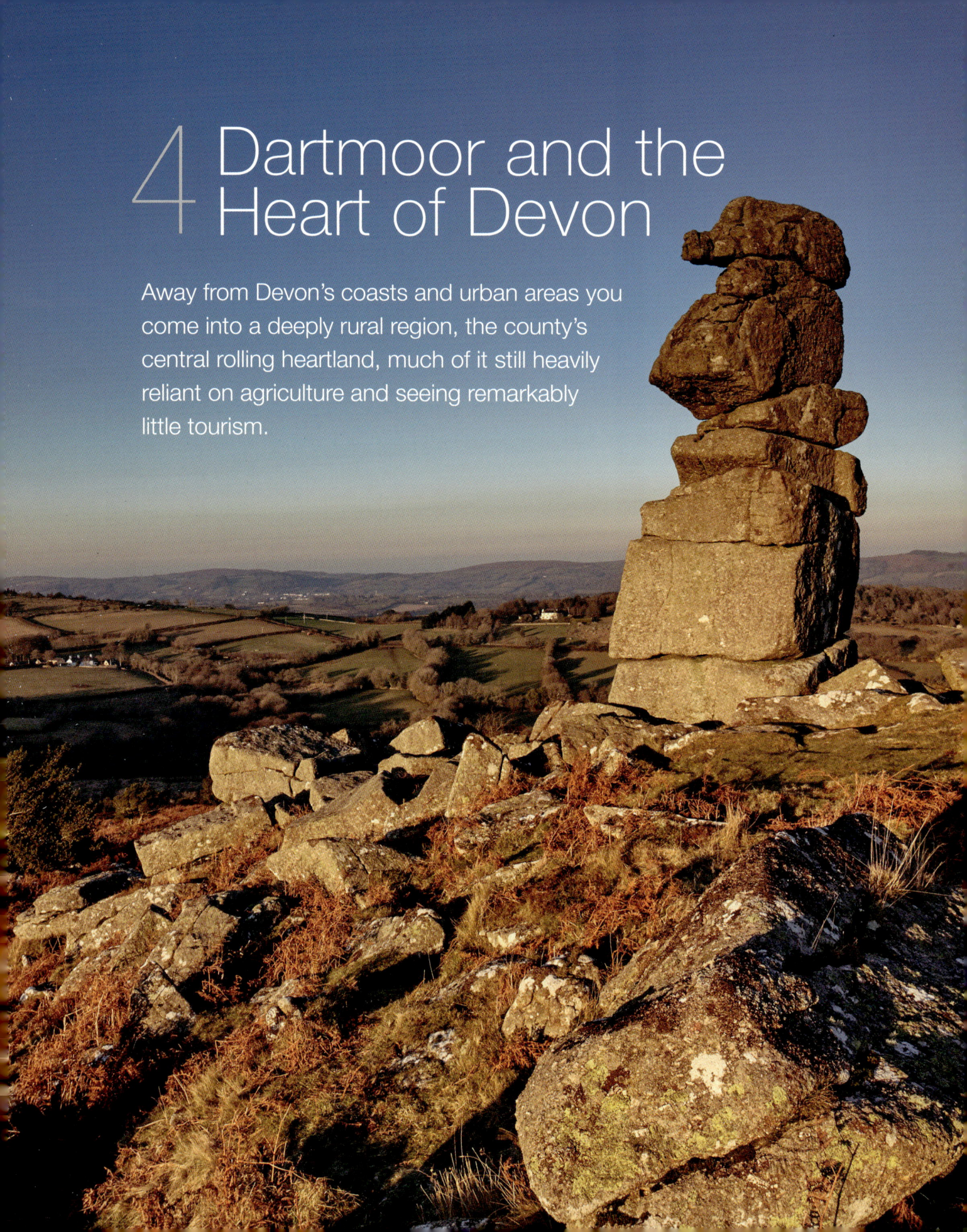

4 Dartmoor and the Heart of Devon

Away from Devon's coasts and urban areas you come into a deeply rural region, the county's central rolling heartland, much of it still heavily reliant on agriculture and seeing remarkably little tourism.

This is a region still rich in Devon's traditions, where rural life remains closely tied to the seasons, and where things move along at their own, less-hurried pace.

The one area that is touched by tourism is of course Dartmoor, the largest of the county's two national parks. Essentially a massive up-welling of granite, its high hills and open moorlands constitute the wildest inland landscapes in the whole of southern England. A characteristic feature of Dartmoor are the tors, massive granite outcrops that form many of the hilltop summits, striking features that define much of the moorland landscape, creating visitor attractions in what can otherwise be quite a bleak landscape.

Rather gentler are the many wooded valleys that have been gouged out of Dartmoor's eastern and southern flanks by the rivers that pour down off the soggy higher moors. The Rivers Dart and Teign in particular have created stunningly beautiful valleys, lined with ancient oak and beech woodlands, refuges to much of the national park's plant and animal wildlife. Both roe and fallow deer are common in these woods, along with otters and dippers along the rivers, accompanied by the ubiquitous badgers and foxes. In terms of plants, bluebells, wild garlic, wood anemone, the true wild daffodil, marsh marigold and bilberry, to name just a few, are all common.

Dartmoor has been settled for several thousand years, and early remnants can still be seen scattered across the landscape in the form of prehistoric village remains, stone circles, burial mounds and field systems. In today's world, a few villages, their buildings hewn out of local granite, lie across the moor, places such as Widecombe-in-the-Moor, Moretonhampstead and Chagford. The main Dartmoor towns, however, lie around its fringes, forming moorland gateways, places such as Okehampton, Bovey Tracey and Tavistock, trading centres that over the centuries prospered on the trade in moorland sheep and their wool, as well as some Dartmoor mining.

Left: Lit by low winter sunlight, Bowerman's Nose, a granite stack on Hayne Down, above the village of Manaton, is one of Dartmoor's iconic landscape features.

Above: Arable farmland in countryside near Tiverton, the heart of rural farming Devon that stretches in a huge swathe across much of the county's inland areas.

To the north of Dartmoor stretches Devon's agricultural heartland, seemingly endless waves of green hills reaching into the far distance, all of them a patchwork of fields, farms, villages and woodlands. Much of the landscape here is quite high, the views reaching far and wide, and the overall feeling one gets is of a remote and depopulated region that has changed remarkably little in a very long time. A few agricultural towns lie scattered across this landscape, places such as Hatherleigh, Winkleigh, South Molton and Crediton, places that are largely devoted to local agriculture and which visitors mainly pass by en route between the moors and the beaches of the north coast.

It is in exactly these quiet green, inland areas that the historic and traditional heart of Devon still beats, well away from the bustle of the main towns and coastal resorts

Beautiful Devon: A Portrait of a County

Above: A solitary gnarled hawthorn tree clings on in open moorland on Sharpitor, a tor standing above Burrator Reservoir in the south of Dartmoor. Hawthorns are one of the very few trees able to survive in the harsh conditions of the open moorland, and it is common to see them standing alone in an otherwise apparently desolate landscape.

Right: The church of Buckfast Abbey, a fully functioning abbey of the Benedictine order. Although the buildings here were completed as recently as 1938, the origins of the abbey go all the way back to 1018, the Saxon period under King Canute. The abbey was dissolved in 1539, under King Henry VIII, and it was not until late in the 19th century when monks returned to reform the abbey, at which time work began to rebuild the abbey we see today. It is said to be the only Medieval monastery in Britain to have been restored to its religious life.

Opposite: The Dart Valley between Dartmeet and Buckfast, in the southern part of Dartmoor, with the River Dart twisting its way southwards towards the sea. The sheltered hillsides are covered with some of Dartmoor's most beautiful and most important ancient oak woodland, something that has given this valley national nature reserve protected status.

Beautiful Devon: A Portrait of a County

Above: The River Dart tumbles over a small waterfall with ancient oak woodland, cloaked in the vibrant greens of early summer, crowding in all around, in the Dart Valley National Nature Reserve, between Dartmeet and New Bridge, in the southern part of Dartmoor.

Right: Thatched cottages nestle in a sheltered and densely wooded valley at Buckland-in-the-Moor, in the southeast of Dartmoor. Thatched cottages are unusual in Dartmoor's generally harsh and windy environment, but these relatively shelterd homes have become quite an iconic Dartmoor view.

Dartmoor and the Heart of Devon

Left: In early May, a beautiful carpet of bluebells - one of the great icons of a British spring - spreads across the woodland floor in Lady's Wood, a nature reserve close to South Brent, on the very southern edge of Dartmoor National Park.

Below: On a snowy winter's day, the old coaching bridge across the West Dart River at Two Bridges, in the heart of Dartmoor, makes for quite a picture postcard view.

Beautiful Devon: A Portrait of a County

Above: The annual Widecombe Fair, a local agricultural show held every September at the Dartmoor village of Widecombe-in-the-Moor, would just not be complete without Uncle Tom Cobley riding his white mare, recalling the words of the ancient song about just this very fair.

Above: Also an essential part of the annual Widecombe Fair are the Morris Dancers and their accompanying musicians, colourfully performing in the main street, just outside the village church.

Left: The upper reach of the North Teign River picks its way over and around a mass of granite boulders as it flows across Gidleigh Common, an expanse of rather desolate open moorland near Chagford, a very typical Dartmoor landscape, seen just before sunset on a late autumn day.

Above: A huge pile of granite boulders consitute Bonehill Rocks, a hillside tor above Widecombe-in-the-Moor, a very typical scene repeated across the hundreds of tors that litter the Dartmoor landscape and which are such an archetypal feature of the national park.

Left: In early summer, a newly opened, vibrantly green fern stands firmly anchored to a moss-covered rock alongside Becka Brook as the stream tumbles over granite boulders close to Becky Falls. The constant spray from these streams provides just the perfect damp environment that these mosses and ferns need to thrive.

Beautiful Devon: A Portrait of a County

Above: Dartmoor is one of the few parts of Devon that can be more or less relied upon to have snow in winter. Although in this scene near Haytor in the moor's northeast the snow is relatively thin - though enough to create quite a magical scene - sometimes the falls are sufficient to cut villages, farms and livestock off from the outside world for several days.

Above: Dartmoor ponies are an utterly iconic feature of Dartmoor - the place simply would not be the same without them - and they are especially beautiful in spring when the mares give birth to their impossibly cute foals.

Right: On a squally autumn day, a fabulous rainbow arches across the moorland of Scorhill Down, near Chagford, coming to Earth right on Scorhill Stone Circle, one of Dartmoor's finest prehistoric remains.

Dartmoor and the Heart of Devon

Beautiful Devon: A Portrait of a County

Above: A wonderfully eccentric display of really quite unusual teapots decorates a wall outside a teashop in Tiverton, helping to draw the attention of potential customers.

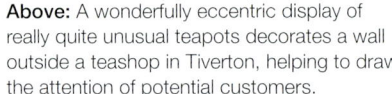

Dartmoor and the Heart of Devon

Left opposite: In springtime a farmer ploughs the red soil of his Devon farm prior to planting, while a host of gulls descends on the newly opened ground to grab whatever food, as worms or insects, that may have been revealed.

Bottom left opposite: In early summer, a couple takes a gentle motorboat trip along the Grand Western Canal, through a verdant bucolic landscape just east of Tiverton.

Left: The rolling agricultural hills of the heart of Devon, in a view seen from the summit of Cadbury Hill, site of a major prehistoric hill fort, a short distance southwest of Bickleigh.

Below: The Fisherman's Cot, an inn sitting on the banks of the River Exe at Bickleigh, a village often considered to be the central point of Devon, seen on a beautiful day in early summer.

Beautiful Devon: A Portrait of a County

Above and insert: The remains of Okehampton Castle on a hillside just west of Okehampton, is the largest castle ruin in Devon. Built shortly after the Norman conquest as a motte-and-bailey castle, it was converted to a residence in the 14th century, before being abandoned in the 16th century.

Right: Old cottages and the church in the centre of Hatherleigh, an historic market and farming town in the heart of Devon, whose economy still revolves very much around the region's agriculture.

Right opposite: The newly rethatched medieval barn at the heart of the walled garden section of the Garden House, a wonderful garden that is largely hidden in the deeply sheltered valleys of the Tamar River, close to the village of Buckland Monachorum, near Tavistock. The barn at one time served as a kitchen for a nearby manor house, but is now largely a decorative part of the walled garden.

Beautiful Devon: A Portrait of a County

Above: In a large marquee a pig happily snoozes while on display at the Okehampton Show, one of Devon's largest agricultural shows, held every August and centred on the farms of Dartmoor and mid-Devon.

Above: David Lamboll, a farmer from south Devon, markets his farm's jams and pickles at the Crediton Farmers' Market, while in the background are the breads of an artesanal baker. With farming becoming increasingly difficult, more and more of Devon's farms are specialising in unusual niche products, as shown by the diversity of products on sale at the county's many farmers' markets.

Right: A pony and trap are taken through their paces in the main ring at the Okehampton Show, one of the most popular events during the show. It reveals the huge, and growing, enthusiasm among the rural community for the recreational driving of horse-drawn carriages of all kinds.

Dartmoor and the Heart of Devon

Left: A row of thatched cottages in the village of Sheepwash, a remarkably remote village in one of the most rural and agricultural parts of mid-Devon. This is a scene that is absolutely typical of many of the small towns and villages of this relatively quiet part of the county, well off the beaten tourist paths of the coasts or even of Dartmoor.

Below: A very wintry, snowbound scene in high countryside near Okehampton, an area prone to harsh weather.

61

5 The North and Devonian Exmoor

The strip of coast and country that we think of as north Devon is very much a microcosm of the county as a whole, squeezing in samples of just about everything that is spread across the rest of the county.

The North and Devonian Exmoor

Huge sandy beaches that are among the southwest's leading surfing venues alternate with some of Devon's most rugged cliffs, while to the east rear up the steep hills and deep valleys of Exmoor. Cutting through it all is one of the area's defining landscape features, the vast Taw and Torridge estuary, the combined outlet for these two north Devon rivers. Much of the countryside is intensely agricultural, with towns and villages scattered across it all, along with a number of quaint coastal fishing coves, honey pots for the huge numbers of summer visitors.

Although most of Exmoor National Park sits within Somerset, the westernmost third slips across the border into Devon, some of the most well known points including the twin villages of Lynton and Lynmouth, along with the nearby wooded Watersmeet valley and the rugged coastal Valley of Rocks. Inland from these, the countryside consists of high rolling hills that are a mixture of enclosed farmland, open moors and the occasional ancient woodland.

Beyond Exmoor's western borders coves and farmland continue, broken only by the towns of Combe Martin and Ilfracombe, until you reach the huge sandy beaches of Woolacombe, Croyde and Saunton Sands, all three major surfing meccas and among North Devon's main visitor draws. All three beaches are backed by dunes, though those behind Saunton are the grand-daddy of them all; Braunton Burrows, one of the largest dune complexes in the UK and home to some very rare plant species. The Burrows also form much of the north shore of the Taw and Torridge estuary, and so are critical to protecting this stretch of calm water from Atlantic storms.

Much of north Devon's urban development is on or around the estuary, Barnstaple and Bideford - the area's largest towns - on the upper reaches of the Taw and Torridge estuaries, respectively, while the pretty villages of Appledore and Instow sit right on the shore of the combined estuary itself.

West of Bideford the landscape starts to become more rugged again, as illustrated by the post-card-perfect fishing village of Clovelly, whose single street seems to descend almost vertically down a slope that is not quite a cliff directly towards the sea. From here, at nearby Hartland Point, the coast takes an abrupt left turn, now facing directly towards the open Atlantic. This is the Hartland coast, a fiercely rugged place of almost sheer cliffs and sharp rocks, the occasional waterfall cascading from cliff-top to shore. Both coast and countryside start to take on a rather wild and battered appearance, before finally crossing the border into Cornwall at the lovely wooded Marsland valley.

Left: A waterfall cascades down a cliff onto the beach, backlit by the early morning sun, at the tiny coastal village of Buck's Mill, between Clovelly and Bideford, on the north Devon coast. Though a lovely location, this shoreline is rather off the beaten track, reachable by just a single, very narrow and steep road.

Above: An early autumn view along the huge sweep of Woolacombe Sands, seen from the village of Mortehoe, with Baggy Point in the far distance. One of north Devon's most magnificent beaches, Woolacombe is also one of the southwest's main surfing spots.

Beautiful Devon: A Portrait of a County

Left: An old dry-stone wall separates farm fields, leading uphill to a solitary ash tree, on one of the highest points of Countisbury Hill, close to the Exmoor coast and high above the town of Lynmouth.

Below: A view across the enormous curve of the Foreland, a headland just east of Lynmouth, on the Exmoor coast, with the Welsh coast in the distance. This view is seen from the earth ramparts of Countisbury Castle, an Iron Age fort built on the summit of the very appropriately named Wind Hill, a place high above the sea and with truly spectacular views.

Opposite: An autumn view of the rugged Exmoor coast, looking west across Wringcliff Bay towards Lee Bay and Woody Bay, seen from the top of the sheer cliffs at the Valley of Rocks, just outside Lynton.

Beautiful Devon: A Portrait of a County

Above: A view near Combe Martin, right on the western edge of Exmoor National Park, of the triangular coastal hill that is Little Hangman, with the hillside continuing to rise up behind it to the mighty Great Hangman, site of some of southern England's highest cliffs.

Above: The River Heddon splashes its way across the pebbly beach at Heddon's Mouth, one of the few truly accessible spots along the remote and rugged Exmoor coast. Even this, however, is reachable only on foot, a one-mile walk after driving to the nearest car park, along some very narrow, remote country lanes.

Above: A group of Exmoor ponies congregates on a remote moorland road. An iconic part of Exmoor, just as Dartmoor ponies are to Dartmoor, they are nevertheless separate breeds. Exmoor ponies are said to be one of the UK's oldest breeds, bred specifically for their hardiness and ability to survive harsh conditions.

The North and Devonian Exmoor

Above: The lovely little Dipper, an iconic species of Exmoor's fast-flowing, clear streams, where it skips from boulder to boulder, dipping its head beneath the water, and often even diving in, swimming underwater to feed on freshwater snails, insect larvae and so on. Usually they are very shy and difficult to watch, but at a few places - such as here at Watersmeet, on the East Lyn River, near Lynmouth - they have become quite used to people.

Right: The white water stream that is Hoar Oak Water pours over a double waterfall, surrounded by dense woodland, just before it joins the East Lyn River, in the lovely wooded valley at Watersmeet.

Above: On a blustery day, the first snows of winter sweep in across the hills of Exmoor's exposed western edge, seen here at Kinsford Gate, near the little village of Brayford.

Beautiful Devon: A Portrait of a County

Above: A dusk and high tide view of the harbour at Ilfracombe. One of north Devon's largest coastal towns and a popular visitor attraction, its harbour is quite definitely the town's most attractive and most easily recognizable feature. The harbour still hosts a small, but active fishing fleet, and it is from here that the ferry to Lundy Island usually sails.

Left: The rugged and rocky shoreline at appropriately named Rockham Bay, leading to the lighthouse at Bull Point, between Ilfracombe and the village of Mortehoe.

The North and Devonian Exmoor

Left: On a warm summer's day, a surfer silhouetted by the afternoon sun rides the Atlantic waves at Croyde Bay, one of north Devon's main surfing beaches.

Below: At low tide, surfers and onlookers at Saunton Sands have a long walk across wet, light-reflecting sand just to reach the water's edge, their silhouettes creating terrific geometric patterns for those with eagle eyes to pick out.

Beautiful Devon: A Portrait of a County

Above: Two very attractive and well cared-for beach huts at the beach resort of Westward Ho!, the only town in the UK to actually have an exclamation mark as part of its name!

Above: Sand dunes line the estuary of the Taw and Torridge Rivers, on the remote shoreline at Crow Point, opposite the harbour town of Appledore.

Above: Shortly before sunset, a pool left behind on Westward Ho!'s sandy beach at low tide, catches the light

The North and Devonian Exmoor

Above: On a windy day, the slowly disintegrating remains of long-lost wooden sea defences get a thorough sand-blasting, on the beach at Crow Point, in the mouth of the Taw and Torridge Rivers. In the far distance surf can be seen pounding a sand bar at the river mouth's outermost seaward limit.

Left: At low tide, an old, wooden gaff-rigged sailing boat, complete with bowsprit, sits on the sand at its mooring close to the lovely riverside town of Instow, in the estuary of the Taw and Torridge Rivers.

Right: The oldest part of Appledore, a small town sitting beside the estuary of the Taw and Torridge Rivers, consists largely of streets lined with Victorian-era terraced cottages. Today, these are mostly used as holiday lets, well maintained and painted in a range of attractive pastel colours.

Beautiful Devon: A Portrait of a County

Above: A pavilion in the formal garden at Tapeley Park, a small stately home and estate near Instow and on a hill above the Torridge estuary..

Above: A scene inside one of Devon's most well known gardens, Rosemoor, which sits in a sheltered valley just outside the town of Great Torrington. Owned by the Royal Horticultural Society (RHS), Rosemoor showcases some of Britain's best horticultural gardening techniques. The garden spreads across quite an area, containing a mix of garden and park types.

Above: Hikers stop to take in the stunning view, atop a granite cliff on Lundy Island's west coast. The whole of Lundy, but especially its west coast, is a wild and rugged place, its cliffs equal to anything in mainland Devon or Cornwall, the island guarding the meeting point of Atlantic Ocean and Bristol Channel.